# Recove
# Broken
# Relationships

Juanita & Dale Ryan

*6 Studies for*
*Groups or Individuals*

With Notes for Leaders

☑ *LIFE RECOVERY GUIDES*

INTERVARSITY PRESS
DOWNERS GROVE, ILLINOIS 60515

*InterVarsity Press® is the book-publishing division of InterVarsity Christian Fellowship®, a student movement active on campus at hundreds of universities, colleges and schools of nursing in the United States of America, and a member movement of the International Fellowship of Evangelical Students. For information about local and regional activities, write Public Relations Dept., InterVarsity Christian Fellowship, 6400 Schroeder Rd., P.O. Box 7895, Madison, WI 53707-7895.*

*All Scripture quotations, unless otherwise indicated, are taken from the HOLY BIBLE, NEW INTERNATIONAL VERSION®. NIV®. Copyright ©1973, 1978, 1984 by International Bible Society. Used by permission of Zondervan Publishing House. All rights reserved.*

*Cover illustration: Tim Nyberg*

*ISBN 0-8308-1165-6*

*Printed in the United States of America* ♾

| 14 | 13 | 12 | 11 | 10 | 9 | 8 | 7 | 6 | 5 | 4 | 3 | 2 | 1 |
|----|----|----|----|----|----|----|----|----|----|----|----|----|----|
| 04 | 03 | 02 | 01 | 00 | 99 | 98 | 97 | 96 | 95 | 94 | 93 | | |

# An Invitation to Recovery

Life Recovery Guides are rooted in four basic convictions.

First, we are in need of recovery. The word *recovery* implies that something has gone wrong. Things are not as they should be. We have sinned. We have been sinned against. We are entangled, stuck, bogged down, bound and broken. We need to be healed.

Second, recovery is a commitment to change. Because of this, recovery is a demanding process and often a lengthy one. There are no quick fixes in recovery. It means facing the truth about ourselves, even when that truth is painful. It means giving up our old destructive patterns and learning new life-giving patterns. Recovery means taking responsibility for our lives. It is not easy. It is sometimes painful. And it will take time.

Third, recovery is possible. No matter how hopeless it may seem, no matter how deeply we have been wounded by life or how often we have failed, recovery is possible. Our primary basis for hope in the process of recovery is that God is able to do things which we cannot do ourselves. Recovery is possible because God has committed himself to us.

Finally, these studies are rooted in the conviction that the Bible can be a significant resource for recovery. Many people who have lived through difficult life experiences have had bits of the Bible thrown at their pain as a quick fix or a simplistic solution. As a result, many people expect the Bible to be a barrier to recovery rather than a resource. These studies are based on the belief that the

Bible is not a book of quick fixes and simplistic solutions. It is, on the contrary, a practical and helpful resource for recovery. We were deeply moved personally by these biblical texts as we worked on this series. We are convinced that the God of the Bible can bring serenity to people whose lives have become unmanageable. If you are looking for resources to help you in your recovery, we invite you to study the Bible with an open mind and heart.

## Getting the Most from Life Recovery Guides

Life Recovery Guides are designed to assist you to find out for yourself what the Bible has to say about different aspects of recovery. The texts you will study will be thought-provoking, challenging, inspiring and very personal. It will become obvious that these studies are not designed merely to convince you of the truthfulness of some idea. Rather, they are designed to allow biblical truths to renew your heart and mind.

We want to encourage realistic expectations of these discussion guides. First, they are not intended to be everything-the-Bible-says about any subject. They are not intended to be a systematic presentation of biblical theology.

Second, we want to emphasize that these guides are not intended to provide a recovery program or to be a substitute for professional counseling. If you are in a counseling relationship or are involved in a support group, we pray that these studies will enrich that resource. If you are not in a counseling relationship and your recovery involves long-term issues, we encourage you to consider seeking the assistance of a mental health professional.

What these guides are designed to do is to help you study a series of biblical texts which relate to the process of recovery. Our hope is that they will allow you to discover the Good News for people who are struggling to recover.

There are six studies in each Life Recovery Guide. This should provide you with maximum flexibility in how you use these guides.

Combining the guides in various ways will allow you to adapt them to your time schedule and to focus on the concerns most important to you or your group.

All of the studies in this series use a workbook format. Space is provided for writing answers to each question. This is ideal for personal study and allows group members to prepare in advance for the discussion. The guides also contain leader's notes with suggestions on how to lead a group discussion. The notes provide additional background information on certain questions, give helpful tips on group dynamics and suggest ways to deal with problems that may arise during the discussion. These features enable someone with little or no experience to lead an effective discussion.

## Suggestions for Individual Study

**1.** As you begin each study, pray that God would bring healing and recovery to you through his Word.

**2.** After spending time in personal reflection, read and reread the passage to be studied.

**3.** Write your answers in the spaces provided or in a personal journal. Writing can bring clarity and deeper understanding of yourself and of the Bible. For the same reason, we suggest that you write out your prayers at the end of each study.

**4.** Use the leader's notes at the back of the guide to gain additional insight and information.

**5.** Share what you are learning with someone you trust. Recovery is empowered by experiences of community.

## Suggestions for Group Study

Even if you have already done these studies individually, we strongly encourage you to find some way to do them with a group of other people as well. Although each person's recovery is different, everyone's recovery is empowered by the mutual support and encouragement that can only be found in a one-on-one or a group setting.

Several reminders may be helpful for participants in a group study:

1. Realize that trust grows over time. If opening up in a group setting is risky, realize that you do not have to share more than what feels safe to you. However, taking risks is a necessary part of recovery. So, do participate in the discussion as much as you are able.

2. Be sensitive to the other members of the group. Listen attentively when they talk. You will learn from their insights. If you can, link what you say to the comments of others so the group stays on the topic. Also, be affirming whenever you can. This will encourage some of the more hesitant members of the group to participate.

3. Be careful not to dominate the discussion. We are sometimes so eager to share what we have learned that we do not leave opportunity for others to respond. By all means participate! But allow others to do so as well.

4. Expect God to teach you through the passage being discussed and through the other members of the group. Pray that you will have a profitable time together.

5. We recommend that groups follow a few basic guidelines, and that these guidelines be read at the beginning of each discussion session. The guidelines, which you may wish to adapt to your situation, are:

　a. Anything said in the group is considered confidential and will not be discussed outside the group unless specific permission is given to do so.

　b. We will provide time for each person present to talk if he or she feels comfortable doing so.

　c. We will talk about ourselves and our own situations, avoiding conversation about other people.

　d. We will listen attentively to each other.

　e. We will be very cautious about giving advice.

　f. We will pray for each other.

If you are the discussion leader, you will find additional suggestions and helpful ideas for each study in the leader's notes. These are found at the back of the guide.

# Recovering from Broken Relationships

Relationships are fragile treasures. They can fail for a variety of reasons. Sometimes misunderstandings tear relationships apart. Sometimes unresolvable conflicts explode between people. Sometimes fears learned in earlier relationships undermine new investments in intimacy. Sometimes a person harms a relationship by cheating or deceit. For these and many other reasons, friendships, business partnerships, marriages and family relationships break apart.

When a significant relationship fails, a part of us dies with it. When our relationships break, our heart also breaks. We grieve. We search for ways to understand what happened. We want to know what went wrong. And we long to find healing for our broken hearts.

It is not easy to trust or to risk intimacy again after we have experienced the pain of a relationship that has failed. When a particular relationship fails, we are tempted to give up on all relationships. We may fear that we will, again, inflict harm or that we will be harmed. We are tempted by the illusion that safety can be found in isolation. The trouble with this strategy, of course, is that we were created to be in relationship. We need other people. Intimate relationships with friends or with family or with a spouse enrich our lives. It is in the context of close relationships that we thrive and grow.

When we experience the trauma of a broken relationship, we need to find healing that corresponds to the depth of the wound. We need to heal so that we can again take the risk to love. This Life Recovery Guide is designed to explore some biblical insights about the process of recovering from the deep wound of a broken relationship—whether that relationship is with a friend, a spouse, a family member or a business associate. Our prayer is that these studies will help you face the painful reality of the losses you have experienced, find healing in God's grace and faithfulness, and learn to love in new ways. It is our prayer that God will heal your broken heart and give you courage to reach out again in love.

*May your roots sink deeply into the soil of God's love.*

*Juanita and Dale Ryan*

# Part 1
## Facing
## Reality

# 1
# Grieving
# the Hurts

*Bill spoke slowly and with obvious difficulty as he explained the* trauma he had experienced in his friendship with Dan. "I have lost both my work and my friend. I can find work again. But how can I replace my lifelong friend?"

Dan and Bill had been business partners for years. Dan designed and oversaw the manufacturing of their product. Bill was in charge of sales. The business grew rapidly. The more success they experienced, however, the more strain developed in their relationship. Although they had been good friends since elementary school, Dan and Bill now seemed to be in conflict about everything. They had very different ideas about how the business should be managed.

Dan began to talk privately with board members and other business associates about Bill. He made it clear that he did not trust Bill and expressed concern that Bill might be intentionally hurting the business. While Bill was out of town on a sales trip, Dan called a board meeting and found a way to take full ownership of the business. Bill returned from his trip to find that he was no longer a full partner in the business. In a single day Bill lost his life's work and his lifelong friendship with Dan.

When a relationship is broken beyond repair, it is like a death. Our only recourse is grief. Grieving is important and necessary, but very painful, work. It is the process of facing the reality of a painful loss and experiencing the strong feelings created by the loss. It is this painful process that makes it possible for us to go on with life.

David experienced this kind of loss in his relationship with King Saul. Once a friend and confidant, Saul turned against David and sought to have him killed. By putting his grief into words, David offers us help in facing our grief over broken relationships.

☐ **Personal Reflection** _____

**1.** What important relationship(s) in your life has failed?

**2.** Briefly describe what happened from your perspective.

**3.** What are your feelings about this loss at this time?

## ☐ Bible Study—————————————————————————————

Listen to my prayer, O God,
   do not ignore my plea;
   hear me and answer me.
My thoughts trouble me and I am distraught
   at the voice of the enemy,
   at the stares of the wicked;
for they bring down suffering upon me
   and revile me in their anger.

My heart is in anguish within me;
   the terrors of death assail me.
Fear and trembling have beset me;
   horror has overwhelmed me.
I said, "Oh, that I had the wings of a dove!
   I would fly away and be at rest—
I would flee far away
   and stay in the desert;
I would hurry to my place of shelter,
   far from the tempest and storm."

If an enemy were insulting me,
   I could endure it;
if a foe were raising himself against me,
   I could hide from him.
But it is you, a man like myself,
   my companion, my close friend,
with whom I once enjoyed sweet fellowship
   as we walked with the throng at the house of God.

Let death take my enemies by surprise;
   let them go down alive to the grave,
   for evil finds lodging among them.

But I call to God,
   and the LORD saves me.
Evening, morning and noon
   I cry out in distress, and he hears my voice. (Psalm 55:1-8, 12-17)

---

**1.** What insights did you gain from your time of personal reflection?

**2.** How does David (the writer) describe the relationship he has lost?

**3.** David says that it would be easier if his enemy, rather than his friend, was the one who was insulting him. Why would this be easier to endure?

**4.** David reacted with intense emotions to his loss. Restate in your own words what he says he is feeling.

**5.** What reaction do you have to this strong expression of emotion?

**6.** How do David's emotions compare with your own?

**7.** David goes through a process of identifying his loss, experiencing strong emotions and asking God for help. This is a good picture of the grief process. What experience have you had with this process?

**8.** The psalmist describes turning to God in his distress. Restate in your own words what he says about this experience.

What experiences have you had with turning to God in your grief?

☐ **Prayer** ————————————————————————————————

What do you want to say to God today about your grief?

# 2
# Seeking Forgiveness from God

*"We were married for ten years." Peter said quietly. "Janet tried a* hundred ways to get me to pay attention to her loneliness. I was so obsessively invested in my work that I couldn't pay attention. My job left little room for anything else in my life—and the truth is that I wanted it like that. I didn't want to feel the painful emotions that came when I slowed down. When Janet asked for time with me, I resented it. And I was afraid. Now I finally understand what was going on. Responsibility is always a complicated thing, but I am now able to focus clearly on my part. I understand my responsibility for the failure of the relationship and my need for forgiveness."

Grieving a lost relationship involves coming to terms with our responsibility for the broken relationship. When we start to face the issue of personal responsibility for a broken relationship, it is important to be cautious not to fall into the trap of blame. Blame is always a simplification. This is true whether we are inclined to blame ourselves or the other person. Healing is not possible until we are able to come to the end of blame and become willing to deal with our side of the problem in appropriate ways. The goal is not to figure out who is to blame for how much of the problem. The goal for this part of our recovery is honesty and the personal growth which honesty makes possible. Our goal is to acknowledge our responsibility for failure, so that we can make appropriate amends and so that we can learn and grow.

When the Scriptures talk about human brokenness it is in the context of God's mercy and forgiveness. It is this context that makes it possible for us to take an honest look at ourselves.

☐ **Personal Reflection** ——————————————————————————————

1. What part do you believe you played in the failure of the relationship you have lost? (If self-blame and over-responsibility are struggles for you, be cautious here. It might be more helpful for you to ask: "What would I do differently if I had it to do again?" or "What is there for me to learn in the failure of this relationship?")

2. What feelings do you have about your contribution to the failure of the relationship?

☐ **Bible Study**————————————————————————————————

Out of the depths I cry to you, O LORD;
  O Lord, hear my voice.

Let your ears be attentive
   to my cry for mercy.

If you, O LORD, kept a record of sins,
   O Lord, who could stand?
But with you there is forgiveness;
   therefore you are feared.

I wait for the LORD, my soul waits,
   and in his word I put my hope.
My soul waits for the Lord
   more than watchmen wait for the morning,
   more than watchmen wait for the morning.

O Israel, put your hope in the LORD,
   for with the LORD is unfailing love
   and with him is full redemption.
He himself will redeem Israel
   from all their sins. (Psalm 130)

---

**1.** What insights did you gain from your time of personal reflection?

**2.** How does the psalmist describe God in this text?

**3.** How does the psalmist describe his emotional state in this text?

**4.** What does the psalmist seem to need from God?

**5.** How do your needs and feelings compare with the needs and feelings expressed by the psalmist?

**6.** What specific forgiveness do you seek from God for the part you played in the failure of your relationship?

**7.** Picture yourself waiting with hope and anticipation for God to forgive you. Picture God coming to you with unfailing love and forgiving you. What thoughts and feelings did you have in response to these images?

8. Are there amends that would be appropriate to make to the other person? If so, what might you say or do?

☐ **Prayer** _____

What feelings do you want to communicate to God today about your broken relationship?

# Part 2
# Healing

# 3
# Accepting
# God's Grace

"*I was so excited when I married Zack,*" began Sally. "*It was my third* marriage. I knew that this time it had to work. I was going to do everything right. But, we ended up getting divorced. 'Three times and you're out,' is what I figure. I am a washout when it comes to marriage. I think it's time for me to give up. I think even God must have given up on me."

When relationships fail, our self-esteem and self-confidence are deeply shaken. We may come to believe that we do not have what it takes to be a friend or a spouse. We may find ourselves thinking and saying terribly negative things about ourselves. We may memorize lists of personal inadequacies and mistakes and recite them silently to ourselves over and over again. We may give up on ourselves and, like Sally, believe that God has given up on us as well.

The Samaritan woman who came to draw water at a well where Jesus was resting had experienced the loss of five marriages. She must have given up on herself as a marriage partner, because when Jesus met her, she was living with a man to whom she was not married. As we will see in the text for this study, this woman may have given up on herself, but God had not given up on her.

God continues to extend his healing grace toward us no matter how many relationships we may have lost.

## ☐ Personal Reflection _____

**1.** What negative thoughts about yourself have you experienced since the loss of your relationship?

**2.** Describe the impact the loss has had on your thoughts and feelings about yourself.

**3.** What effect has your loss had on other existing or potential relationships?

## ☐ Bible Study_____

Jacob's well was there, and Jesus, tired as he was from the journey, sat down by the well. It was about the sixth hour.

When a Samaritan woman came to draw water, Jesus said to her, "Will you give me a drink?" (His disciples had gone into the town to buy food.)

The Samaritan woman said to him, "You are a Jew and I am a Samaritan woman. How can you ask me for a drink?" (For Jews do not associate with Samaritans.)

Jesus answered her, "If you knew the gift of God and who it is that asks you for a drink, you would have asked him and he would have given you living water."

"Sir," the woman said, "you have nothing to draw with and the well is deep. Where can you get this living water? Are you greater than our father Jacob, who gave us the well and drank from it himself, as did also his sons and his flocks and herds?"

Jesus answered, "Everyone who drinks this water will be thirsty again, but whoever drinks the water I give him will never thirst. Indeed, the water I give him will become in him a spring of water welling up to eternal life."

The woman said to him, "Sir, give me this water so that I won't get thirsty and have to keep coming here to draw water."

He told her, "Go, call your husband and come back."

"I have no husband," she replied. Jesus said to her, "You are right when you say you have no husband. The fact is, you have had five husbands, and the man you now have is not your husband. What you have just said is quite true."

"Sir," the woman said, "I can see that you are a prophet." (John 4:6-19)

---

1. What insights did you gain from your time of personal reflection?

**2.** What was the woman's initial reaction to Jesus' request for a drink?

**3.** How do you think this woman felt about herself as a result of her gender, her ethnic identity and her relationship history?

**4.** How would you describe Jesus' interaction with this woman?

**5.** What is the significance of what Jesus offered this woman?

**6.** In what way do you identify with this woman?

**7.** Jesus offered many gifts of grace to this woman. What have you experienced of Jesus' gifts of grace in your life?

What barriers keep you from receiving these gifts of grace?

**8.** Picture yourself sitting with Jesus. You expect to be judged and rejected. Instead, Jesus reaches out to you and engages you in a dialogue. He offers you living water. He knows you well, your strengths and your failings. Yet, without hesitation, he offers you his grace and love. What thoughts and feelings do you have in response to this meditation?

☐ **Prayer** _____

What would you like to say to the God who offers you healing grace?

# 4
# Experiencing God's Faithfulness

"When my fiancée broke off our engagement and then married some-one else almost immediately, I was devastated," John said through his tears. "It felt like my life was over. I was adopted at the age of five after being bounced around between several foster homes. But I never felt like I really belonged in the family that adopted me. So, this relationship was my first hope for a real home, a place where I could finally belong. When it came to an end, it felt like all my hopes for a home and a future came to an end as well. The hardest part was that it felt like God had abandoned me as well."

When an important relationship fails, it often feels as if we are being forsaken by God. This might not make sense to our logical, cognitive self—we may still affirm God's faithfulness and commit-ment to us. But our relationship with God is an intimate relation-ship—it involves more than just our intellectual affirmations about God. Even though we may believe in God's love and care, we may feel abandoned. The Bible is very clear that God is close to the brokenhearted. But when we are brokenhearted, we rarely experi-ence this in the ways we would prefer.

Part of the healing we need as we recover from a broken relationship is to experience God's faithfulness to us. God will not leave us or forget us. When our losses overwhelm us we can turn to God for comfort and compassion. God promises never to forget us.

## ☐ Personal Reflection _____

**1.** What negative impact has the loss of your relationship had on your relationship with God?

**2.** What positive impact has the loss of your relationship had on your relationship with God?

## ☐ Bible Study_____

Shout for joy, O heavens;
    rejoice, O earth;
    burst into song, O mountains!
For the LORD comforts his people
    and will have compassion on his afflicted ones.

But Zion said, "The LORD has forsaken me,
    the Lord has forgotten me."

"Can a mother forget the baby at her breast
   and have no compassion on the child she has borne?
Though she may forget,
   I will not forget you!
See, I have engraved you on the palms of my hands;
   your walls are ever before me." (Isaiah 49:13-16)

---

**1.** What insights did you gain from your time of personal reflection?

**2.** God's people have gone through a very traumatic experience before the writing of this text. They feel that God has forgotten them.
What is it about difficult or traumatic times, such as the loss of a
relationship, that can cause us to question God's presence?

**3.** God responds in this text with three reassuring images. In the
first image we are presented with a picture of a mother with a
nursing infant and asked, "Can a mother forget her child?" What
thoughts and feelings do you have in response to this image of God?

This text clearly suggests that mothers were intended to be attentive and nurturing toward their dependent children. How does this compare to your experience as a child?

**4.** The second reassuring image in this text is that of being engraved on the palms of God's hands. What does this image convey?

What meaning does this image have for you?

**5.** The third reassuring image in this text is of God paying constant attention to our "walls." What meaning does this image have in the text?

What is the meaning of this image to you?

**6.** The opening of this text describes the joy that comes when we experience comfort and compassion from God. The mountains burst into song because God comforts the afflicted. What feelings do you experience when you are comforted by a compassionate friend?

What feelings do you experience when you are comforted and reassured by God?

**7.** Write a brief, honest prayer to the God who "comforts his people" and who has "compassion on his afflicted ones."

8. Choose one of the images in this text. Meditate on the image. Think of the meaning the image has for you. Allow yourself to picture God's compassionate attention to you in the life situations you currently face. What feelings and thoughts did you have during this meditation?

☐ **Prayer** _____

What would you like to say to the God who promises never to forget you?

# Part 3
# Risking
# Love Again

# 5
# Growing in the Capacity to Love

*"What is love anyway?" Sharon asked with a sharp edge of anger in* her voice. "Is there really such a thing? Or is it just some cheap word we fling around? If there is such a thing, maybe the problem is that we are all too self-centered, too broken, too sinful to be able to love. Maybe love is an impossibility."

Sharon had experienced a series of broken friendships. Two close friends had recently moved to other states and for months neither had written or called. Another friend had betrayed her by inappropriately sharing information about Sharon with a mutual acquaintance. Sharon was deeply wounded by these losses and broken trust. Her parents had said the words "I love you" to her, but they showed little interest in her other than to criticize her. Now her friends, who said they cared about her, were behaving as if they did not. Love suddenly seemed like an empty word to Sharon. Why risk loving again if it is doomed to failure?

But love is not an empty word. Love is at the heart of what is real because God is love. God assures us that we are loved. We can learn from God what it means to truly love so that we can risk loving again.

## ☐ Personal Reflection _____

**1.** List five behaviors that effectively communicate to you: "I love you."

**2.** List five ways you commonly express love to someone else.

**3.** How would you define or describe love in one or two sentences?

## ☐ Bible Study_____

If I speak in the tongues of men and of angels, but have not love, I am only a resounding gong or a clanging cymbal. If I have the gift of prophecy and can fathom all mysteries and all knowledge, and if I have a faith that can move mountains, but have not love, I am nothing. If I give all I possess to the poor and surrender my body to the flames, but have not love, I gain nothing.

Love is patient, love is kind. It does not envy, it does not boast, it is not proud. It is not rude, it is not self-seeking, it is not easily angered, it keeps no record of wrongs. Love does not delight in evil but rejoices with the truth. It always protects, always trusts, always hopes, always perseveres. (1 Corinthians 13:1-7)

---

**1.** What insights did you gain from your time of personal reflection?

**2.** The text begins by comparing the relative value and importance of love. To what does the text compare love?

What does the text say about the importance of love in comparison with these other things?

How could spiritual giftedness and self-sacrificing behaviors actually be harmful without love?

**3.** Make a list of all the things the text says love is not.

**4.** How might each of these behaviors harm a relationship?

**5.** Make a list of all the things the text says love is.

**6.** How might each of these behaviors contribute to a relationship?

**7.** Which of the negative characteristics are problems for you in relationships? Explain.

**8.** Which of the positive characteristics are strengths you bring to relationships? Explain.

**9.** Describe how you would like to grow and change in your ability to love.

☐ **Prayer** _____

What would you like to say to the God of love about your desire to grow in your capacity to love?

# 6
# Nurturing New Relationships

*"I just don't think I have what it takes to start over,"* Paul sighed. "This whole process has left me feeling like I don't have the skills or the know-how to sustain a close relationship with anyone. I expect nothing but more failure. And that means that I will get hurt again and someone else will also get hurt."

When a relationship fails we are left with the twin demons of grief and fear. It will not be easy to find the courage to invest again in intimacy. It is understandably frightening to invest time and energy in a relationship knowing that there is a possibility for failure. It can be terrifying to be vulnerable enough to expose our hearts and to let ourselves care deeply for someone again.

As we work through the grief and the fear, however, we will experience opportunities to nurture new relationships. These are opportunities to grow in many ways. As we will see in this text, it is an opportunity to grow in the virtues of compassion, kindness, humility, gentleness, patience, forgiveness and gratitude.

## ☐ Personal Reflection _____

1. What fears do you have as you enter new relationships?

2. What hopes do you have as you enter new relationships?

## ☐ Bible Study_____

Therefore, as God's chosen people, holy and dearly loved, clothe yourselves with compassion, kindness, humility, gentleness and patience. Bear with each other and forgive whatever grievances you may have against one another. Forgive as the Lord forgave you. And over all these virtues put on love, which binds them all together in perfect unity. Let the peace of Christ rule in your hearts, since as members of one body you were called to peace. And be thankful. Let the word of Christ dwell in you richly as you teach and admonish one another with all wisdom, and as you sing psalms, hymns and spiritual songs with gratitude in your hearts to God. And whatever you do, whether in word or deed, do it all in the name of the Lord Jesus, giving thanks to God the Father through him. (Colossians 3:12-17)

1. What insights did you gain from your time of personal reflection?

**2.** The text encourages us to clothe ourselves with compassion, kindness, humility, gentleness and patience. What contribution does each of these virtues make to a relationship?

**3.** Pick two or three of these virtues, and describe how they are demonstrated in healthy relationships.

**4.** Which of these are strengths for you? Explain.

Which are especially difficult? Explain.

**5.** The text also encourages us to bear with each other and forgive whatever grievances we may have against one another. How would bearing with each other and forgiving grievances contribute to a relationship?

**6.** What difficulties do you experience with forgiving grievances?

**7.** Are there limits to what we are being asked to "bear with"? Explain.

**8.** The text also encourages us to have a grateful spirit. "Be thankful . . . sing . . . with gratitude in your hearts to God . . . giving thanks." How does gratitude contribute to our relationships?

□ **Prayer** _____

What help would you like to ask from God as you begin to nurture new relationships?

# Leader's Notes

You may be experiencing a variety of feelings as you anticipate leading a group using a Life Recovery Guide. You may feel inadequate for the task and afraid of what will happen. If this is the case, know you are in good company. Many of the kings, prophets and apostles in the Bible felt inadequate and afraid. Many other small group leaders share this experience of fear as well.

Your willingness to lead, however, is a gift to the other group members. It might help if you tell them about your feelings and ask them to pray for you. Keep in mind that the other group members share the responsibility for the group. And realize that it is God's work to bring insight, comfort, healing and recovery to group members. Your role is simply to provide guidance to the discussion. The suggestions listed below will help you to provide that guidance.

## Using the Life Recovery Guides

This Life Recovery Guide is one in a series of guides. The series was designed to be a flexible tool that can be used in various combinations by individuals and groups—such as support groups, Bible studies and Sunday-school classes. All of the guides in this series are designed to be useful to anyone. Each guide has a specific focus, but all are written with a general audience in mind.

Many congregation-based recovery ministries use the Life Recovery Guides as part of the curriculum for "newcomers" groups. It can be a critical step in the recovery process to recognize that "recovery" is not a new set of ideas or the latest trend in popular psychology. Finding that the Bible is attentive to our struggles can often provide the courage needed to continue when the journey becomes painful.

We strongly recommend that careful attention be given to the group dynamics of the Bible study. Traditional Bible studies in the Christian community tend to be cognitively oriented, leadership tends to be well defined, commenting on statements by other participants is usually encouraged, giving advice is often valued, and sharing concerns expressed in the group with nonparticipants is often understood to be a kind of caring. Special attention will often be needed, therefore, to use the Life Recovery Guides in a way that teaches group participants the norms, values and group dynamics of the support group ministry to which the person is being introduced.

For example, if the Life Recovery Guides are used as an introductory experience that leads toward participation in a Twelve-Step group, then the group dynamics should probably resemble as much as possible those of a Twelve-Step group. Group facilitators should take time to carefully explain the purpose of the group and to introduce group participants to new group norms. It will probably take some time and practice, for example, to assimilate the concept of "cross talk." Groups using the Life Recovery Guides can help build a biblical foundation for what follows in the recovery process. But they can also help people to develop the skills needed to benefit from a support group experience.

Each guide contains six studies. If eight guides are used, they can provide a year-long curriculum series. Or if the guides are used in pairs, they can provide studies for a quarter (twelve weeks). The following are some ways that you might find it helpful to use the guides in combination with one another:

| Topic | Number of Studies/Weeks | Guides to Use |
|---|---|---|
| **Introduction to Recovery** | 12 | Recovery from Distorted Images of God<br>Recovery from Distorted Images of Self |
| **Abuse** | 30 | Recovery from Abuse<br>Recovery from Shame<br>Recovery from Distorted Images of Self<br>Recovery from Fear<br>Recovery from Spiritual Abuse |
| **Addictions** | 30 | Recovery from Addictions (Steps 1-3)<br>Recovery from Guilt (Steps 4-9)<br>Recovery: A Lifelong Journey (Steps 10-12)<br>Recovery from Codependency<br>Recovery from Workaholism |
| **Family Dysfunctions** | 18 | Recovery from Family Dysfunctions<br>Recovery from Distorted Images of God<br>Recovery from Distorted Images of Self |
| **Divorce** | 30 | Recovery from Depression<br>Recovery from Loss<br>Recovery from Shame<br>Recovery from Broken Relationships<br>Recovery from Bitterness |
| **Grief and Loss** | 24 | Recovery from Loss<br>Recovery from Fear<br>Recovery from Depression<br>Recovery from Distorted Images of God |

## Preparing to Lead

**1.** Develop realistic expectations of yourself as a small group leader. Do not feel that you have to "have it all together." Rather, commit yourself to an ongoing discipline of honesty about your own needs. As you grow in honesty about your own needs, you will grow as well in your capacity for compassion, gentleness and patience with yourself and with others. As a leader, you can encourage an atmosphere of honesty by being honest about yourself.

**2.** Pray. Pray for yourself and your own recovery. Pray for the group members. Invite the Holy Spirit to be present as you prepare and as you meet.

**3.** Read the study several times.

**4.** Take your time to thoughtfully work through each question, writing out your answers.

**5.** After completing your personal study, read through the leader's notes for the study you are leading. These notes are designed to help you in several ways. First, they tell you the purpose the authors had in mind while writing the study. Take time to think through how the questions work together to accomplish that purpose. Second, the notes provide you with additional background information or comments on some of the questions. This information can be useful if people have difficulty understanding or answering a question. Third, the leader's notes can alert you to potential problems you may encounter during the study.

**6.** If you wish to remind yourself during the group discussion of anything mentioned in the leader's notes, make a note to yourself below that question in your study guide.

### Leading the Study

**1.** Begin on time. You may want to open in prayer, or have a group member do so.

**2.** Be sure everyone has a study guide. Decide as a group if you want people to do the study on their own ahead of time. If your time together is limited, it will be helpful for people to prepare in advance.

**3.** At the beginning of your first time together, explain that these studies are meant to be discussions, not lectures. Encourage the members of the group to participate. However, do not put pressure on those who may be hesitant to speak during the first few sessions. Clearly state that people do not need to share anything they do not feel safe sharing. Remind people that it will take time to trust each other.

**4.** Read aloud the group guidelines listed in the front of the guide. These commitments are important in creating a safe place for people to talk and trust and feel.

**5.** The covers of the Life Recovery Guides are designed to incorporate both symbols of the past and hope for the future. During your first meeting, allow the group to describe what they see in the cover and respond to it.

**6.** Read aloud the introductory paragraphs at the beginning of the discussion for the day. This will orient the group to the passage being studied.

**7.** The personal reflection questions are designed to help group members focus on some aspect of their experience. Hopefully, they will help group members to be more aware of the frame of reference and life experience which they bring to the study. The personal reflection section can be done prior to the group meeting or as the first part of the meeting. If the group does not prepare in advance, approximately ten minutes will be needed for individuals to consider these questions.

The personal reflection questions are not designed to be used directly for group discussion. Rather, the first question in the Bible study section is intended to give group members an opportunity to reveal what they feel safe sharing from their time of personal reflection.

**8.** Read the passage aloud. You may choose to do this yourself, or prior to the study you might ask someone else to read.

**9.** As you begin to ask the questions in the guide, keep several things in mind. First, the questions are designed to be used just as they are written. If you wish, you may simply read them aloud to the group. Or you may prefer to express them in your own words. However, unnecessary rewording of the questions is not recommended.

Second, the questions are intended to guide the group toward understanding and applying the main idea of the study. You will find the purpose of each study described in the leader's notes. You should try to understand how the study questions and the biblical text work together to lead the group in that direction.

There may be times when it is appropriate to deviate from the study guide. For example, a question may have already been answered. If so, move on to the next question. Or someone may raise an important question not covered in the guide. Take time to discuss it! The important thing is to use discretion. There may be many routes you can travel to reach the goal of the study. But the easiest route is usually the one we have suggested.

**10.** Don't be afraid of silence. People need time to think about the question before formulating their answers.

**11.** Draw out a variety of responses from the group. Ask, "Who else has some thoughts about this?" or "How did some of the rest of you respond?" until several people have given answers to the question.

**12.** Acknowledge all contributions. Try to be affirming whenever possible. Never reject an answer. If it seems clearly wrong to you, ask, "Which part of the text led you to that conclusion?" or "What do the rest of you think?"

**13.** Realize that not every answer will be addressed to you, even though this will probably happen at first. As group members become more at ease, they will begin to interact more effectively with each other. This is a sign of a healthy discussion.

**14.** Don't be afraid of controversy. It can be very stimulating. Differences can enrich our lives. If you don't resolve an issue completely, don't be frustrated. Move on and keep it in mind for later. A subsequent study may resolve the problem. Or, the issue may not be resolved—not all questions have answers!

**15.** Stick to the passage under consideration. It should be the source for answering the questions. Discourage the group from unnecessary cross-referencing. Likewise, stick to the subject and avoid going off on tangents.

**16.** Periodically summarize what the group has said about the topic.

This helps to draw together the various ideas mentioned and gives continuity to the study. But be careful not to use summary statements as an opportunity to give a sermon!

**17.** During the discussion, feel free to share your own responses. Your honesty about your own recovery can set a tone for the group to feel safe in sharing. Be careful not to dominate the time, but do allow time for your own needs as a group member.

**18.** Each study ends with a time for prayer. There are several ways to handle this time in a group. The person who leads each study could lead the group in a prayer or you could allow time for group participation. Remember that some members of your group may feel uncomfortable about participating in public prayer. It might be helpful to discuss this with the group during your first meeting and to reach some agreement about how to proceed.

**19.** Realize that trust in a group grows over time. During the first couple meetings, people will be assessing how safe they will feel in the group. Do not be discouraged if people share only superficially at first. The level of trust will grow slowly but steadily.

## Listening to Emotional Pain

Life Recovery Guides are designed to take seriously the pain and struggle that is part of life. People will experience a variety of emotions during these studies. Your role as group leader is not to act as a professional counselor. Instead it is to be a friend who listens to emotional pain. Listening is a gift you can give to hurting people. For many, it is not an easy gift to give. The following suggestions can help you listen more effectively to people in emotional pain.

**1.** Remember that you are not responsible to take the pain away. People in helping relationships often feel that they are being asked to make the other person feel better. This is usually related to the helper's own patterns of not being comfortable with painful feelings.

**2.** Not only are you not responsible to take the pain away, one of the things people need most is an opportunity to face and to experience the pain in their lives. They have usually spent years denying their pain and running from it. Healing can come when we are able to face our pain in the presence of someone who cares about us. Rather than trying to take the pain away, commit yourself to listening attentively as it is expressed.

**3.** Realize that some group members may not feel comfortable with expressions of sadness or anger. You may want to acknowledge that such emotions are uncomfortable, but remind the group that part of recovery is to learn to feel and to allow others to feel.

**4.** Be very cautious about giving answers and advice. Advice and answers may make you feel better or feel competent, but they may also minimize people's problems and their painful feelings. Simple solutions rarely work, and they can easily communicate "You should be better now" or "You shouldn't really be talking about this."

**5.** Be sure to communicate direct affirmation any time people talk about their painful emotions. It takes courage to talk about our pain because it creates anxiety for us. It is a great gift to be trusted by those who are struggling.

The following notes refer to the questions in the Bible study portion of each study:

### Study 1. Grieving the Hurts. Psalm 55:1-8, 12-17.

*Purpose:* To understand the need to face the hurts and grieve the losses of a broken relationship.

**Question 2.** He says that the person who is now insulting him and raising himself against him was once his companion, his close friend, a man like himself, with whom he enjoyed sweet fellowship.

**Question 3.** There are at least two reasons why being hurt by an enemy is less painful than being hurt by a friend. First, when an enemy hurts us, it is what we expect to happen. We are unprepared for insults from a friend. Second, when an enemy hurts us there is no loss of relationship, because we do not have a close relationship with an enemy. When a friend hurts us and the relationship is broken, we experience a significant loss.

**Question 5.** Some people may feel relieved that such intense feelings can be expressed. Others might be quite frightened by such intense feelings—especially the anger. If these expressions of anger are frightening, it might be useful to explore the sources of the fear. Often, people who have experienced verbal or physical abuse, or who have witnessed it, can be frightened when they experience anger in themselves or others. It is important to note that David was given an opportunity to kill Saul, but did not do so. Expressing our anger to God is not the same as acting on it. David asks God to be responsible for putting things right. He expresses his anger to God and, in doing so, lets go and does not take matters into his own hands.

**Question 6.** The strong feelings that come with grief include the entire range of human emotional experience. People may feel fear, anxiety, anguish, sorrow, longing, guilt, self-blame, rage, hatred, confusion, insecurity, depression, vindictiveness and/or hopelessness. These feelings need to be acknowledged and expressed in some way (not necessarily with the person involved, but in prayer or with a trusted friend, pastor or counselor). Putting these emotions into words provides a road map to healing from loss. The emotions are there to help us take in the reality and the personal significance of the loss we have experienced. They may show us other losses that we have not yet grieved or resolved. If these feelings are buried, they will be buried alive and can grow into bitterness and paralyzing fear. Access to the feelings that come with grief and healing can only happen in the context of a caring relationship. We are wounded in relationships, we heal in relationships. Because many of us come from families that did not understand or value the grief process, many of us have been shamed for feeling and expressing grief. As a result it may be very difficult to experience the strong emotions of grief. If this is the case for you, it will be particularly important to spend some time talking with a pastor or counselor or trusted friend who will not shame you for your feelings, but who will give you permission to experience and express your feelings.

**Question 8.** David says, "I call to God all day and all night. God hears me when I call out to him and he helps me in my distress."

### Study 2. Seeking Forgiveness from God. Psalm 130.

*Purpose:* To explore personal responsibility and need for change in the context of God's mercy and forgiveness.

**Question 2.** God is described as a forgiving God, as a God of unfailing love and as a God who offers full redemption.

**Question 3.** The psalmist is crying to God "out of the depths." He is waiting for God to respond to him with forgiveness. It is clear that the psalmist is deeply distressed by his sin. He is eager to talk with God about it and to experience God's forgiveness.

**Question 4.** The psalmist needs mercy and forgiveness from God. God's forgiveness is the basis of the psalmist's hope. If God were not forgiving, if he "kept a record of sins, who could stand?"

**Question 8.** Amends are primarily verbal acknowledgments of our harmful behaviors. Amends involve specific descriptions of these behaviors and a statement of our sorrow for having caused the other person harm. The focus needs to be kept on our part of the problem. The point is not to get the other person to respond in any way (not even to say, "I forgive you"). The point is to acknowledge our wrongdoing and, when possible, to take steps to put things right. (For a fuller disussion of amend-making, see *Recovery from Guilt.*)

### Study 3. Accepting God's Grace. John 4:6-19.

*Purpose:* To experience God's healing grace when faced with the shame of a broken relationship.

**Question 2.** The woman was surprised that Jesus interacted with her. The social norms of the day made her an inferior, both as a woman and because of her social class (a Samaritan). The woman would have expected Jesus to ignore her—to act as if she were not there. Instead, Jesus asked her for assistance.

**Question 3.** In all probability each of these factors contributed to low self-esteem. She probably felt the sting of prejudice and rejection on a daily basis. All of this no doubt contributed to a poor self-concept.

**Question 4.** Jesus talked to this woman the way he talked to his disciples or to anyone. He did not treat her as an inferior. His interactions with her were respectful and gentle.

**Question 5.** Jesus offered her living water. It is an offer of abundant life and of eternal life. He also offered her knowledge about himself as the Messiah. Jesus extended his grace, his kindness, his forgiveness and his hope toward this woman. Jesus did not participate in discrimination against her for reasons of race, gender or personal failure in life.

### Study 4. Experiencing God's Faithfulness. Isaiah 49:13-16.

*Purpose:* To remember God's commitment to never leave us or forsake us.

**Question 2.** Sometimes it does not make sense to us that God can be loving and powerful and, yet, painful things happen to us. We do not comprehend why God does not protect us from evil. One way of "making sense" out of this difficulty is to determine that God is inattentive or forgetful. If we have had experiences in the past with significant people in our lives abandoning us physically or emotionally, we will be particularly susceptible to experiencing God as absent. It is a very frightening experience to feel that God has forgotten us. We depend on God for our very life, just as we depended on our parents when we were very young. We need reassurance that God will not forget us, or we will worry about our very survival.

**Question 3.** The first thing that may strike people is that God is pictured here as female. God is our mother. The second striking thing for some people may be that they answer "yes" to this seemingly rhetorical question. They may have felt in one way or another that they were "forgotten" by their mother. The third striking reality is that God is a mother who will not forget her children, but will care for them and be responsive to their needs. There are many ways that people are "forgotten" by their mothers. Mothers may die, or become ill, or be depressed, or be alcoholic, or give their child up for adoption, or leave home, or have too many other pressing concerns, or lack the emotional capacity to nurture a child. If a person experienced being "forgotten" by their mother, this image will have a powerful meaning. It may be difficult to believe that God will be responsive to our needs because that does not correspond with our experience in the first years of life.

**Question 4.** When words are engraved in flesh, they are permanent. And when words are on the palms of the hands, they will be seen many times a day. God is saying it will be impossible, no matter what, for us to be forgotten. It is the permanency of this image that is so powerful. Nothing can undo our relationship with God. Most of us have experienced conditional love. We would be loved and valued if . . . we were funny, or smart, or good, or quiet, or compliant. If we stop doing what is expected of us, we fear losing the love or attention we so desperately seek. God's love is not conditional. God will not get rid of us or reject us.

**Question 5.** The survival of a city in the psalmist's day depended on the city wall. An unattended wall meant vulnerability to one's enemies. The image emphasizes God's attentiveness to our needs for boundaries. God seeks to protect us—our walls are "ever before him." The phrase "ever before me" suggests that God always sees us, we never leave his sight. He never turns away from us. He sees and knows and understands everything.

### Study 5. Growing in the Capacity to Love. 1 Corinthians 13:1-7.

*Purpose:* To learn from Scripture what it means to love.

**Question 2.** The text tells us in dramatic terms that (1) being very gifted spiritually (with knowledge or faith or special abilities) or (2) being extremely self-sacrificing (to the point of dying) is not as important as being a loving person. In fact, this text tells us that if we are spiritually gifted or self-sacrificing but do not have love, our gifts and sacrifices are worthless. Without love, spiritual giftedness leads to spiritual arrogance and judgmentalism, which can be deadly to other people's spiritual well-being. Without love, self-sacrificing behaviors can become a manipulative ploy to induce false guilt in others and thus control their behavior.

**Question 3.** Love does not envy, does not boast, is not proud, is not rude, is not self-seeking, is not easily angered, does not keep record of wrongs, does not delight in evil.

**Question 5.** Love is patient, is kind, rejoices in the truth, protects, trusts, hopes and perseveres.

### Study 6. Nurturing New Relationships. Colossians 3:12-17.

*Purpose:* To explore ways to nurture new relationships.

**Question 2.** Compassion brings an understanding perspective to a relationship. It helps us to keep in mind that the other person is wounded and struggling in life just as we are. Kindness gives us the ability to reach out to the other person with a desire to be responsive to his or her needs. Humility gives us an awareness of our limits. It reminds us that we are not superior, that we are finite, that we also have needs. Gentleness keeps us approachable and vulnerable, making intimacy more possible. Patience gives us the wisdom of timing. We do not have to be in a hurry; we do not get anything in a relationship by being demanding or by rushing things.

**Question 3.** Compassion is demonstrated through empathic listening and warmth. Kindness is demonstrated through thoughtful acts. Gentleness is demonstrated through verbal and physical affection and the exercise of caution when angry. Humility is demonstrated through an ability to be honest about our needs and limits. Patience is demonstrated through long-term commitment—not running when things get difficult.

**Question 5.** Forgiveness and "bearing with each other" are important to relationships because it is inevitable that we will hurt each other. We fail. We blow it. This is reality. We are all wounded human beings who wound each other. We cannot have lasting relationships unless we know this and know that we will have to forgive ourselves and the other person. Forgiveness, however, does not mean that we are to pretend that everything is fine when it is not. Forgiveness is not a bandage. It is a process. Forgiveness involves (1) facing the hurt we have experienced, (2) talking about the hurt, (3) feeling whatever we feel, (4) trying to solve whatever problems are involved, (5) asking for what we need, (6) accepting the other person's limits and (7) letting go of the hurt and of our demands.

**Question 7.** It is an abuse of the biblical injunctions to forgive to suggest that people in abusive situations should "bear with" whatever comes their way. We do not violate the biblical injunction to "bear with" when we tell the truth, when we hold people accountable for their actions or when we protect ourselves from abusive situations.

**Question 8.** Gratitude helps us to receive good things from the other person. It helps us to take in the good gifts God gives us through others. In this way, gratitude leads to joy.

*For more information about Christian resources for people in recovery and subscription information for* STEPS, *the newsletter of the National Association for Christian Recovery, we invite you to write to:*

*The National Association for Christian Recovery*
*P.O. Box 11095*
*Whittier, California 90603*

# LIFE RECOVERY GUIDES FROM INTER-VARSITY PRESS
*By Dale and Juanita Ryan*

*Recovery from Abuse.* Does the nightmare of abuse ever end? After emotional, verbal and/or physical abuse how can you develop secure relationships? Recovery is difficult but possible. This guide will help you turn to God as you put the broken pieces of your life back together again. Six studies, 64 pages, 1158-3.

*Recovery from Addictions.* Addictions have always been part of the human predicament. Chemicals, food, people, sex, work, spending, gambling, religious practices and more can enslave us. This guide will help you find the wholeness and restoration that God offers to those who are struggling with addictions. Six studies, 64 pages, 1155-9.

*Recovery from Bitterness.* Sometimes forgiveness gets blocked, stuck, restrained and entangled. We find our hearts turning toward bitterness and revenge. Our inability to forgive can make us feel like spiritual failures. This guide will help us find the strength to change bitterness into forgiveness. Six studies, 64 pages, 1154-0.

*Recovery from Broken Relationships.* Divorce. Family conflict. Death. We may learn to fear closeness because we don't want to experience another separation from someone we love. God wants to heal us of the pain of lost relationships. These studies help us discover how to risk love again and build healthy relationships that will endure. Six studies, 64 pages, 1165-6.

*Recovery from Codependency.* The fear, anger and helplessness people feel when someone they love is addicted can lead to desperate attempts to take care of, or control, the loved one. Both the addicted person's behavior and the frenzied codependent behavior progress in a destructive downward spiral of denial and blame. This guide will help you to let go of over-responsibility and entrust the people you love to God. Six studies, 64 pages, 1156-7.

*Recovery from Depression.* From time to time we all experience feelings of hopelessness in response to difficult events in life—broken relationships, death, unemployment and so on. Sometimes we are not able to work through those feelings alone. And we need to be pointed toward the source of hope. This guide will show you the way. Six studies, 64 pages, 1161-3.

*Recovery from Distorted Images of God.* In a world of sin and hate it is difficult for us to understand who the God of love is. These distortions interfere with our ability to express our feelings to God and to trust him. This guide helps us to identify the distortions we have and to come to a new understanding of who God is. Six studies, 64 pages, 1152-4.

*Recovery from Distorted Images of Self.* God created us as people who are to be loved, valued and capable. But sometimes we don't *feel* that we are really cared for. We mentally replay negative feedback again and again. These studies will show you how to escape those negatives and be restored to a true vision of yourself as a person of immense worth. Six studies, 64 pages, 1162-1.

*Recovery from Family Dysfunctions.* Dysfunctional patterns of relating learned early in life affect all of our relationships. We trust God and others less than we wish. This guide offers healing from the pain of the past and acceptance into God's family. Six studies, 64 pages, 1151-6.

*Recovery from Fear.* Our fears revolve around certain basic issues—intimacy, risk, failure, loneliness, inadequacy and danger. But God offers us support, empowerment and courage to face fear in all areas of life. This guide will help us discover how God can enable us to face our fears. Six studies, 64 pages, 1160-5.

*Recovery from Guilt.* Guilt is a distress signal that warns us that something is wrong. If we do not pay attention, we will continue in destructive ways. This guide offers help in working through the pain of what we have done to ourselves and others. Using steps four through nine of the Twelve Steps in conjunction with Scripture, these studies offer hope and help to get beyond guilt to forgiveness. Six studies, 64 pages, 1163-X.

*Recovery: A Lifelong Journey.* Recovery requires a commitment to keep growing and changing through prayer and discipline. In this guide you'll see how the last three steps of the Twelve Steps provide a model for your lifelong journey of recovery. By following the disciplines of self-awareness, confession, seeking God and asking for guidance, you will find continued healing and growth. Six studies, 64 pages, 1166-4.

*Recovery from Loss.* Disappointment, unmet expectations, physical or emotional illness and death are all examples of losses that occur in our lives. Working through grief does not help us to forget what we have lost, but it does help us grow in understanding, compassion and courage in the midst of loss. This guide will show you how to receive the comfort God offers. Six studies, 64 pages, 1157-5.

*Recovery from Shame.* Shame is a social experience. Whatever its source, shame causes people to see themselves as unlovable, unworthy and irreparable. This guide will help you to reform your self-understanding in the light of God's unconditional acceptance. Six studies, 64 pages, 1153-2.

*Recovery from Spiritual Abuse.* Because of negative teaching we have received, many of us have learned that we have to earn our way with God. We have come to experience the Christian life as a burden—and a source of deep shame. Through these studies, we will discover that we can be healed of spiritual abuse and find freedom and grace in Christ. Six studies, 64 pages, 1159-1.

*Recovery from Workaholism.* Hard work results in promotions, raises and the respect of colleagues. More important, it fills the need we have to be needed. But overwork also eats away at marriage and family relationships, while making friendships outside the office nearly non-existent. It can create health problems as well as spiritual struggles. This guide is designed to help you break free of workaholism and accept the rest that God offers. Six studies, 64 pages, 1164-8.